PRINCEWILL LAGANG

Relationships in the Modern World:
Challenges and Solutions

First published by PRINCEWILL LAGANG 2023

Copyright © 2023 by Princewill Lagang

All rights reserved. No part of this publication may be reproduced, stored or transmitted in any form or by any means, electronic, mechanical, photocopying, recording, scanning, or otherwise without written permission from the publisher. It is illegal to copy this book, post it to a website, or distribute it by any other means without permission.

Princewill Lagang has no responsibility for the persistence or accuracy of URLs for external or third-party Internet Websites referred to in this publication and does not guarantee that any content on such Websites is, or will remain, accurate or appropriate.

First edition

This book was professionally typeset on Reedsy.
Find out more at reedsy.com

Contents

1	Introduction	1
2	The Digital Age and Communication	3
3	Balancing Personal and Professional Lives	6
4	Navigating Social Media and Jealousy	9
5	Intimacy in the Age of Distraction	12
6	Modern Dating Dynamics	15
7	Multicultural and Interfaith Relationships	18
8	Long-Distance Relationships in the Modern Era	21
9	Self-Care and Mental Health in Relationships	24
10	Gender Roles and Equality in Modern Relationships	27
11	Coping with Relationship Pressures	30
12	The Future of Relationships	33

1

Introduction

In an ever-evolving world, the dynamics of human relationships have taken center stage, showcasing the intricate interplay of emotions, communication, and connection. This book delves into the complexities of relationships in the modern era, unraveling the multifaceted nature of human interactions.

As we navigate the 21st century, relationships have been profoundly impacted by the rapid changes that characterize our times. Technological advancements, shifting societal norms, and the globalization of cultures have given rise to both opportunities and challenges in the realm of relationships. What once followed traditional paths and predictable trajectories now encounters a landscape defined by uncertainty, diversity, and the blending of various cultural and ideological backgrounds.

The complexities of modern relationships are mirrored in the various forms they take. Long gone are the days of a singular definition of partnership; instead, we witness an array of relationship types, from long-distance connections nurtured through screens to unconventional partnerships that challenge established norms. The advent of social media and online dating platforms has further reshaped the way individuals meet and interact, adding layers of complexity to the journey of forming meaningful bonds.

In this era, relationships must grapple with the paradox of hyper-connectivity and genuine emotional disconnection. The constant influx of information and the pressure to present curated versions of ourselves online often obscure the authentic experiences that form the foundation of deep connections. Navigating the boundary between the virtual and the real has become an intricate dance, raising questions about vulnerability, trust, and intimacy.

The challenges that modern relationships face are as diverse as the relationships themselves. Communication, once limited by physical presence, is now extended across digital platforms, testing our ability to convey emotions, interpret cues, and sustain meaningful dialogue. Cultural clashes, fueled by the globalization of societies, introduce new layers of complexity to relationships, demanding open-mindedness and adaptability.

This book aims to dissect these intricate layers, offering insights into the evolving landscape of modern relationships. Through a combination of research, real-life stories, and practical advice, we will explore the various dimensions that relationships encompass today. By delving into the challenges, opportunities, and nuances that define modern connections, we hope to provide a comprehensive understanding of how relationships are forged, tested, and nurtured in this complex era.

As we embark on this journey through the intricate web of modern relationships, it's essential to recognize that the path ahead is both exciting and uncertain. The chapters that follow will delve into specific aspects of these relationships, shedding light on the emotions, psychology, and strategies that can guide individuals through the maze of contemporary connections.

2

The Digital Age and Communication

In an era dominated by technology, the way we communicate has undergone a profound transformation, leaving an indelible mark on the landscape of relationships. Chapter 2 explores the intricate interplay between the digital age and communication within relationships, delving into both the advantages and challenges posed by our hyper-connected world.

The Impact of Technology on Communication:

Technology has not only revolutionized the speed and accessibility of communication but has also fundamentally altered its nature. The ability to instantly connect across distances, facilitated by smartphones, social media, and messaging platforms, has collapsed geographical boundaries and allowed relationships to flourish across continents. However, this ease of connection has come with its own set of complexities.

Benefits of Staying Connected in a Digital World:

The digital age has bestowed relationships with an unprecedented level of connectivity. Couples separated by miles can share their daily lives, exchange messages, and participate in each other's experiences as if they were in the same room. This instant accessibility can foster a sense of intimacy and closeness that was once challenging to maintain in long-distance relationships.

Moreover, the digital realm offers an array of tools that enable partners to express themselves creatively and thoughtfully. Emojis, GIFs, and multimedia messages allow for a nuanced exchange of emotions that can transcend the limitations of plain text. Additionally, social media platforms provide a window into each other's lives, enabling partners to share moments, milestones, and aspirations, further deepening their bond.

Challenges of Communication in a Digital World:

Despite the benefits, the digital age has introduced its fair share of challenges to communication within relationships. The instantaneous nature of messaging can lead to misunderstandings, as nuances and context often get lost in text-based exchanges. The absence of nonverbal cues such as tone of voice and facial expressions can create ambiguity and misinterpretation, potentially leading to conflicts.

Moreover, the constant barrage of notifications and alerts from various digital platforms can foster a sense of distraction and detachment, diverting attention away from meaningful interactions. The pressure to curate an idealized online persona can also result in a lack of authenticity, hindering genuine communication and vulnerability.

Striking a Balance:

Navigating the digital age's impact on communication requires a delicate balance. Partners must consciously allocate time for quality interactions, both online and offline, ensuring that the digital world complements rather than replaces face-to-face conversations. Establishing boundaries around device usage during specific moments, such as meals or intimate discussions, can help maintain a deeper connection.

Furthermore, open dialogue about the challenges posed by technology is crucial. Acknowledging the potential pitfalls of digital communication and sharing concerns about its impact on the relationship can lead to mutual understanding and joint efforts to address these issues.

In conclusion, Chapter 2 underscores the dual nature of the digital age's impact on communication within relationships. While technology offers unprecedented connectivity and creative expression, it also presents challenges that demand mindfulness, authenticity, and open communication. Striking a balance between the benefits and pitfalls of the digital world is essential for fostering healthy, meaningful connections in this complex era.

3

Balancing Personal and Professional Lives

In the modern world, the pursuit of ambitious career goals often intersects with the desire for fulfilling personal relationships. Chapter 3 delves into the intricate dance of balancing personal and professional lives within relationships, examining the challenges that arise and presenting strategies to navigate this delicate equilibrium.

Challenges of Maintaining Work-Life Balance:

The demands of a fast-paced professional life can exert significant strain on relationships. Long working hours, unpredictable schedules, and the ever-present connectivity of technology can blur the lines between work and personal time. This blurring can lead to feelings of neglect, frustration, and a sense of emotional disconnection within relationships.

Furthermore, the pressure to excel in one's career can inadvertently lead to neglecting one's own well-being and the needs of a partner. This imbalance can create tension, impacting the emotional intimacy and mutual support that relationships thrive on.

Strategies for Juggling Career and Relationships:

1. Open Communication: Clear and honest communication is the foundation of navigating this challenge. Partners should openly discuss their career aspirations, schedules, and expectations for personal time. Sharing concerns about work-related stress and its impact on the relationship can foster understanding and support.

2. Boundaries: Establishing boundaries between work and personal life is essential. Designating specific times for personal interactions, date nights, and relaxation can help prevent work from encroaching on relationship time. Similarly, creating dedicated spaces for work and leisure at home can signal a shift in focus.

3. Prioritization: Regularly reassess priorities and goals. Partners should collaboratively identify what matters most to each of them and find ways to accommodate each other's aspirations. This might involve compromising on certain career pursuits to ensure the relationship remains a central focus.

4. Quality Over Quantity: While spending ample time together is valuable, the quality of that time matters equally. Engaging in meaningful conversations, shared activities, and experiences can foster a deeper connection even in limited timeframes.

5. Self-Care: Both partners should prioritize self-care, recognizing that maintaining their own well-being directly impacts the health of the relationship. This might involve setting aside time for personal hobbies, exercise, and relaxation.

6. Delegating and Outsourcing: When possible, delegate or outsource tasks that consume time and energy. This can help free up space for both career and relationship commitments.

7. Flexibility: Embrace flexibility in both professional and personal spheres. Unforeseen events may disrupt schedules, and being adaptable can ease stress and prevent unnecessary conflicts.

Creating a Synergy:

The key to successfully balancing personal and professional lives within relationships lies in creating a synergy between the two. Partners must recognize that they are allies in supporting each other's growth and well-being. By aligning their goals, communication, and efforts, they can navigate the challenges and opportunities presented by their individual pursuits.

Ultimately, striking a balance between career ambitions and relationship commitments requires a blend of understanding, compromise, and conscious effort. This chapter emphasizes that, with effective communication, mutual support, and the implementation of thoughtful strategies, individuals can thrive both professionally and personally while nurturing a healthy and fulfilling relationship.

4

Navigating Social Media and Jealousy

In an era defined by connectivity, the influence of social media on relationships has become undeniable. Chapter 4 delves into the intricate relationship between social media and jealousy within partnerships, dissecting the impact of virtual connections and offering strategies to manage jealousy while fostering trust and mutual understanding.

The Impact of Social Media on Relationships:

Social media platforms have reshaped how we interact, connect, and present ourselves to the world. While they offer opportunities for self-expression and communication, they can also introduce complexities into relationships. The curated nature of online personas, coupled with the ability to reconnect with past flames or form new connections, can ignite feelings of jealousy and insecurity.

Triggers for Jealousy:

The virtual world amplifies the potential for jealousy to take root. Seeing partners interacting with others online, exchanging likes and comments, or connecting with ex-partners can spark feelings of inadequacy or mistrust. The phenomenon of "micro-cheating," where seemingly innocent interactions with others online trigger jealousy, adds to the challenges couples face.

Strategies for Managing Social Media and Jealousy:

1. Open Dialogue: Start with open conversations about the role of social media in your relationship. Discuss your feelings, concerns, and boundaries related to online interactions. Establishing a shared understanding can help prevent misunderstandings.

2. Set Boundaries: Define healthy boundaries for online interactions. This might involve agreeing on what's acceptable in terms of interacting with ex-partners, sharing personal information, and engaging with new connections.

3. Practice Empathy: Put yourself in your partner's shoes. Consider how your online actions might be perceived and how they align with your partner's feelings. Empathy can foster understanding and minimize unintended triggers.

4. Limit Online Checking: Resist the urge to constantly monitor your partner's online activity. Excessive checking can lead to mistrust and anxiety. Trust is essential for a healthy relationship.

5. Prioritize Real Moments: Allocate time for meaningful offline interactions. Engaging in shared activities, deep conversations, and quality time can reinforce the bond you share in the real world.

6. Share Offline Activities Online: Celebrate your relationship by sharing genuine moments online. This can include photos, experiences, and milestones that showcase the authenticity of your connection.

7. Practice Self-Reflection: Reflect on your own triggers and insecurities.

Understand that jealousy often stems from personal feelings and experiences that may not be related to your partner's actions.

8. Support Each Other's Online Interactions: Instead of viewing each other's online connections as threats, be supportive of their individual networks. Encourage each other's interests and friendships.

Cultivating Trust in the Digital Age:

Navigating social media and managing jealousy in relationships requires a conscious effort to cultivate trust. Trust is built on open communication, transparency, and a shared commitment to the relationship's well-being. By acknowledging the potential triggers of jealousy and working collaboratively to establish boundaries and communication norms, couples can leverage the benefits of social media while safeguarding their emotional connection.

In essence, Chapter 4 highlights that, in a world driven by virtual connections, nurturing trust and managing jealousy are essential for maintaining a healthy and harmonious relationship. The digital realm can enhance our lives, but it's vital to remember that the foundation of any strong partnership lies in genuine, offline interactions and the trust that underpins them.

5

Intimacy in the Age of Distraction

In a world brimming with constant distractions, the delicate flame of intimacy and emotional connection within relationships often finds itself at risk. Chapter 5 delves into the profound impact of distractions on intimacy and explores strategies to rekindle, nurture, and sustain the essential bonds that underpin relationships.

The Effects of Distractions on Intimacy:

In the age of digital devices, notifications, and competing demands for attention, carving out space for intimate moments can become a challenging feat. Distractions can erode the quality of interactions, leading to surface-level conversations and emotional disconnection. The lure of virtual spaces can divert attention away from the present moment and hinder the deep, genuine connections that intimacy thrives on.

Rekindling Intimacy:

1. Mindful Presence: Practice being fully present during interactions. Put away devices, maintain eye contact, and actively engage in conversations.

This simple act can create a sense of connection that transcends distractions.

2. Scheduled Quality Time: Allocate dedicated time for each other, free from distractions. Schedule regular date nights, walks, or activities that encourage uninterrupted conversation and shared experiences.

3. Digital Detox: Occasionally disconnect from digital devices and social media. Engage in offline activities that allow you to connect on a deeper level, whether it's cooking together, exploring new hobbies, or simply enjoying nature.

4. Expressing Gratitude: Share appreciations and expressions of gratitude. These acknowledgments can reinforce the emotional connection and remind both partners of their value in each other's lives.

5. Physical Touch: Physical touch is a powerful vehicle for intimacy. Embrace cuddling, holding hands, and other forms of non-sexual touch to foster closeness and emotional connection.

Sustaining Intimacy:

1. Emotional Vulnerability: Encourage open sharing of feelings and thoughts. Vulnerability cultivates intimacy by allowing partners to see and understand each other's authentic selves.

2. Deep Conversations: Engage in conversations that go beyond the surface. Discuss dreams, fears, and aspirations, creating a safe space for exploring the depths of each other's minds.

3. Shared Rituals: Establish meaningful rituals that are unique to your relationship. Whether it's a weekly movie night, a morning coffee together, or a monthly adventure, these shared experiences can deepen your connection.

4. Spontaneous Affection: Surprise each other with spontaneous acts of affection. These gestures can remind both partners of the spark that ignited their relationship.

5. Active Listening: Truly listen when your partner speaks. Avoid thinking about your response while they talk, and instead, focus on understanding their perspective.

Cultivating Intimacy Amidst Distractions:

Intimacy thrives when nurtured within the context of shared experiences, vulnerability, and mutual understanding. While distractions are omnipresent, their influence can be mitigated by deliberate actions that prioritize the relationship. By embracing mindfulness, intentional communication, and shared moments of genuine connection, couples can overcome the challenges posed by distractions and create a rich tapestry of intimacy that enriches their lives.

In essence, Chapter 5 underscores that maintaining intimacy in the age of distraction requires conscious effort and a commitment to being present for each other. By reclaiming moments of quality interaction, fostering emotional openness, and embracing shared experiences, couples can cultivate a strong foundation of intimacy that endures despite the noise of the digital world.

6

Modern Dating Dynamics

In the digital era, the landscape of dating and courtship has evolved significantly, reshaping the way individuals form connections and navigate relationships. Chapter 6 delves into the intricacies of modern dating, exploring the impact of technology on romantic interactions and providing valuable advice for successfully navigating the realm of online dating while managing expectations.

Changing Landscape of Dating:

The rise of technology has brought both convenience and complexity to the realm of dating. Online platforms and apps have expanded the pool of potential partners, enabling individuals to connect with others across distances and demographics. However, this virtual landscape also introduces challenges such as deciphering digital signals, managing rejections, and fostering genuine connections amidst the noise.

Navigating Online Dating:

1. Authentic Profile Presentation: When creating an online dating profile,

aim for authenticity. Genuine photos and an honest description of yourself can attract partners who appreciate you for who you are.

2. Clear Communication: Engage in open and transparent communication from the beginning. Express your intentions, preferences, and values to ensure you're on the same page with potential matches.

3. Take Time to Know: Invest time in getting to know each other before meeting in person. Engage in meaningful conversations to assess compatibility beyond surface-level interests.

4. Balancing Texting and Real Interaction: While texting can establish a connection, aim to meet in person relatively early to gauge chemistry and compatibility beyond virtual interactions.

Managing Expectations:

1. Realistic Expectations: Recognize that online profiles provide limited insights into a person's full personality. Avoid building unrealistic expectations based solely on appearances or written descriptions.

2. Navigating Rejections: Rejections are a natural part of dating. Approach them with resilience and remember that compatibility is a two-way street.

3. Communication Over Assumption: If uncertain about someone's intentions, communicate openly. Assumptions can lead to misunderstandings and unnecessary complications.

4. Healthy Pace: Take time to develop a connection. Avoid rushing into intense commitments too soon; allow the relationship to unfold naturally.

5. Personal Growth: Approach dating as an opportunity for personal growth and learning. Each interaction, whether successful or not, can offer valuable

insights about yourself and your preferences.

Balancing Digital and Real-World Interactions:

1. Transition to Real Interaction: Once a connection is established, transition from digital interactions to real-world dates. Face-to-face conversations provide a deeper understanding of each other.

2. Avoid Overanalysis: Avoid dissecting every text or message. Overanalyzing can lead to unnecessary stress and misinterpretation.

3. Trust Your Intuition: Listen to your gut feelings. If something doesn't feel right, it's important to prioritize your well-being.

Embracing the Journey:

Modern dating dynamics require a blend of patience, self-awareness, and adaptability. While technology can facilitate connections, nurturing a meaningful relationship still relies on genuine interactions, shared experiences, and effective communication. By navigating the digital landscape with authenticity and a balanced perspective, individuals can forge connections that hold the potential for lasting love and companionship.

In essence, Chapter 6 underscores that modern dating is a dynamic journey that demands self-awareness, clear communication, and a willingness to embrace both the opportunities and challenges presented by technology. By approaching dating as a process of self-discovery and relationship-building, individuals can navigate the digital realm while cultivating connections that have the potential to thrive in the real world.

7

Multicultural and Interfaith Relationships

In an interconnected world, relationships frequently transcend cultural and religious boundaries, creating diverse and enriching partnerships. Chapter 7 delves into the complexities of multicultural and interfaith relationships, exploring the challenges these partnerships may encounter and offering strategies for fostering understanding, respect, and harmony.

Challenges of Multicultural and Interfaith Relationships:

Navigating the intricacies of multicultural and interfaith relationships can be both rewarding and challenging. While such relationships offer the opportunity to learn from and celebrate different perspectives, they also involve reconciling varying traditions, beliefs, and expectations. Challenges can arise from differing values, communication styles, and cultural norms, and they may be intensified by external pressures and societal expectations.

Rewards and Opportunities:

Multicultural and interfaith relationships provide a unique chance to broaden one's horizons, expand cultural knowledge, and deepen empathy. Partners learn to appreciate the richness of each other's backgrounds, fostering a deeper connection that transcends mere physical attraction. Such relationships can also contribute to personal growth, as individuals develop the ability to navigate differences with sensitivity and grace.

Strategies for Fostering Understanding and Harmony:

1. Open Dialogue: Establish open and respectful communication from the beginning. Encourage discussions about cultural and religious beliefs, values, and expectations. This shared understanding forms the foundation for a harmonious relationship.

2. Cultural Exchange: Embrace the opportunity to learn about each other's cultures and faiths. Participate in cultural events, festivals, and traditions, fostering a deeper appreciation for your partner's background.

3. Respectful Curiosity: Approach discussions with curiosity rather than judgment. Ask questions to gain insight into your partner's perspective, and actively listen to their experiences.

4. Common Values: Identify shared values that transcend cultural or religious differences. These commonalities can provide a strong basis for your relationship's growth.

5. Boundary Setting: Establish boundaries that respect both partners' cultural and religious sensitivities. Discuss potential challenges that might arise and create strategies for addressing them.

6. Seek Support: Seek guidance from multicultural or interfaith support groups, counselors, or clergy members. They can offer advice and tools for navigating complex issues.

7. Flexibility: Be willing to compromise and adapt. Flexibility and

compromise are essential in any relationship, but they become even more vital in multicultural and interfaith partnerships.

8. Embrace Individuality: Recognize that your partner's background is an integral part of their identity. Encourage their individuality and celebrate their uniqueness.

Embracing the Complexity:

Multicultural and interfaith relationships demand patience, empathy, and a willingness to learn and grow together. By fostering an environment of mutual respect, open communication, and a shared commitment to understanding, couples can navigate the intricacies of diverse partnerships and create a harmonious blend of traditions and beliefs.

In essence, Chapter 7 underscores that multicultural and interfaith relationships are a celebration of diversity and an opportunity for personal and relational growth. By embracing the complexities and challenges with an open heart and mind, partners can create a tapestry of understanding and harmony that reflects the beauty of their shared journey.

8

Long-Distance Relationships in the Modern Era

In an era marked by global mobility and interconnectedness, long-distance relationships have become increasingly common. Chapter 8 delves into the intricacies of maintaining love and connection across geographical divides, examining the prevalence of long-distance relationships in today's world and exploring how technology can both assist and complicate the effort to stay connected.

The Prevalence of Long-Distance Relationships:

Globalization, career opportunities, and educational pursuits often lead individuals to form relationships that span cities, countries, or continents. The prevalence of long-distance relationships highlights the commitment, trust, and emotional resilience required to sustain connections when physical presence is limited.

The Role of Technology:

Technology has reshaped the landscape of long-distance relationships, providing tools that bridge gaps and facilitate communication. Video calls, instant messaging, and social media platforms offer real-time interaction, making it possible to share experiences and emotions despite being miles apart. However, the role of technology is multifaceted, and it can introduce its own set of challenges.

Benefits of Technology in Long-Distance Relationships:

1. Virtual Presence: Technology allows partners to maintain a sense of presence in each other's lives. Video calls, photos, and updates provide glimpses into daily routines and experiences.

2. Real-Time Communication: Instant messaging and video calls enable partners to stay in touch in real time, bridging the gap created by physical distance.

3. Shared Activities: Online platforms facilitate shared activities, such as watching movies together or playing online games, creating a sense of connection despite the miles.

Challenges Introduced by Technology:

1. Miscommunication: Text-based communication can lead to misunderstandings due to the absence of nonverbal cues and tone. What seems harmless in text might be misconstrued.

2. Overreliance on Technology: Relying solely on technology for communication might lead to a lack of depth in conversations. Partners might avoid addressing deeper emotions or concerns.

3. Time Zone Differences: Time zone disparities can complicate scheduling conversations and finding mutually convenient times to connect.

LONG-DISTANCE RELATIONSHIPS IN THE MODERN ERA

Strategies for Navigating Long-Distance Relationships:

1. Communication Routines: Establish regular communication routines, whether through scheduled calls, daily messages, or shared experiences.

2. Quality Over Quantity: Prioritize quality conversations over constant communication. Meaningful interactions foster a deeper connection.

3. Visits and Plans: Plan visits and set goals for eventual reunions. Having tangible plans for the future can provide hope and a shared sense of purpose.

4. Honesty and Transparency: Share your feelings openly, including any challenges or insecurities you're experiencing. Honesty builds trust and understanding.

5. Embrace Independence: While maintaining a strong connection is essential, also focus on personal growth and interests.

Balancing Technology and Authentic Connection:

In a world where technology both bridges and separates, long-distance relationships require intentionality and balance. While virtual interactions can provide a lifeline across distances, they should be complemented by the anticipation of in-person reunions and a commitment to fostering authentic emotional connection.

Chapter 8 underscores that, in the modern era, long-distance relationships can thrive when partners use technology as a tool for connection, while also recognizing its limitations. By embracing clear communication, planning visits, and focusing on quality interactions, couples can maintain a strong bond despite the physical miles that separate them.

9

Self-Care and Mental Health in Relationships

A mid the intricacies of modern relationships, the chapter of self-care and mental health takes center stage. Chapter 9 delves into the vital role that self-care and mental well-being play in sustaining healthy relationships. It explores the significance of nurturing individual wellness and provides insights into how partners can support each other's emotional health within the context of their relationship.

The Importance of Self-Care:

Maintaining a healthy relationship starts with caring for oneself. Self-care encompasses physical, emotional, and mental well-being. When individuals prioritize their own health and happiness, they are better equipped to contribute positively to the partnership.

The Connection between Mental Health and Relationships:

Mental well-being directly influences relationship dynamics. Unaddressed stress, anxiety, or emotional struggles can lead to communication breakdowns, heightened conflict, and emotional distancing. Conversely, individuals who prioritize their mental health tend to bring greater emotional balance and stability to their relationships.

Strategies for Prioritizing Self-Care:

1. Recognize Individual Needs: Understand your own needs and practice self-awareness. Regularly assess how you're feeling emotionally and physically.

2. Establish Boundaries: Set boundaries that protect your mental well-being. Communicate your limits and make time for activities that rejuvenate you.

3. Nurture Physical Health: A healthy body contributes to a healthy mind. Prioritize regular exercise, balanced nutrition, and adequate sleep.

4. Practice Mindfulness: Engage in mindfulness techniques such as meditation, deep breathing, or journaling to manage stress and maintain emotional balance.

5. Pursue Hobbies: Engaging in hobbies and activities that bring joy and fulfillment can boost overall well-being.

6. Seek Professional Help: If facing mental health challenges, consider seeking support from a therapist, counselor, or mental health professional.

Supporting Each Other's Mental Health:

1. Open Dialogue: Encourage conversations about mental well-being. Create a safe space where both partners can share their thoughts, feelings, and challenges.

2. Active Listening: When your partner opens up, actively listen without

judgment. Offer empathy and support.

3. Offer Encouragement: Recognize and acknowledge your partner's efforts toward self-care. Offer words of encouragement and validation.

4. Joint Self-Care: Engage in self-care activities together, such as practicing mindfulness, going for walks, or cooking healthy meals.

5. Share Responsibilities: Distribute household and relationship responsibilities to prevent either partner from feeling overwhelmed.

6. Respect Boundaries: Understand and respect each other's boundaries. Be attuned to signs of emotional stress and support each other accordingly.

Cultivating Emotional Well-Being Together:

The journey of self-care and mental well-being is intertwined with the journey of a relationship. Partners who prioritize their individual emotional health contribute positively to the partnership's overall vitality. By nurturing self-care habits and offering unwavering support, couples can cultivate a relationship space that values authenticity, empathy, and mutual well-being.

Chapter 9 underscores that nurturing mental health and practicing self-care are integral to sustaining a healthy, thriving relationship. When both partners prioritize emotional well-being, they create a resilient foundation that allows love, understanding, and support to flourish.

10

Gender Roles and Equality in Modern Relationships

The ever-evolving dynamics of gender roles have cast a transformative light on modern relationships. Chapter 10 delves into the intricate tapestry of shifting gender roles, exploring their impact on relationships and emphasizing the significance of communication and collaboration in the journey towards achieving equality within partnerships.

Shifting Gender Roles:

The traditional paradigms of gender roles have undergone a profound shift, with women and men redefining their roles in society. Women's empowerment, increasing opportunities for education and career advancements, and changing societal norms have contributed to the transformation of expectations and dynamics within relationships.

Impact on Modern Relationships:

The evolution of gender roles has redefined the landscape of modern relationships, challenging traditional notions of who performs which roles and responsibilities. While this shift has opened doors for more egalitarian relationships, it can also lead to misunderstandings and conflicting expectations if not navigated consciously.

Importance of Communication:

Open communication is a cornerstone of navigating evolving gender roles. Partners should engage in candid discussions about their respective expectations, preferences, and the roles they envision within the relationship. This proactive approach prevents assumptions and misunderstandings, fostering a more harmonious connection.

Collaboration for Equality:

1. Shared Responsibilities: Partners should jointly determine how household, financial, and familial responsibilities are divided. Recognize that these decisions should be based on individual strengths, interests, and circumstances.

2. Flexible Roles: Embrace flexibility in roles and responsibilities. Strive to create a dynamic where both partners contribute to tasks that align with their abilities and interests, rather than adhering to rigid gender-based expectations.

3. Supporting Career Aspirations: Acknowledge and support each other's career aspirations. Celebrate accomplishments and navigate decisions about work-life balance together.

4. Embracing Emotions: Encourage emotional openness in both partners. Men and women should feel free to express their feelings without conforming to traditional stereotypes.

5. Parenting as Partners: Approach parenting as equal partners, sharing

responsibilities and decisions related to child-rearing.

Challenges and Growth:

While striving for gender equality within relationships is a noble goal, it doesn't come without challenges. Societal expectations, internalized beliefs, and external pressures can influence individuals' perceptions of roles and responsibilities. However, navigating these challenges can lead to profound personal and relational growth.

Fostering a Balanced Connection:

Chapter 10 underscores the significance of embracing evolving gender roles and working collaboratively to achieve equality within relationships. By fostering open communication, recognizing the value of each partner's contributions, and encouraging shared decision-making, couples can create a foundation that not only celebrates individuality but also nurtures a balanced and harmonious connection.

11

Coping with Relationship Pressures

In a world heavily influenced by societal and cultural expectations, the pressures that bear upon relationships can be significant. Chapter 11 delves into the complexities of managing external pressures and offers strategies to navigate these challenges while nurturing the core of the partnership.

Understanding Societal and Cultural Pressures:

Societal and cultural norms often shape our perceptions of relationships, dictating expectations about marriage, parenthood, career choices, and more. These external pressures can introduce tension and stress into relationships, as partners strive to meet or defy these expectations.

Impact on Relationships:

The weight of societal and cultural pressures can lead to disagreements, feelings of inadequacy, and even the erosion of intimacy. The tension between individual desires and external expectations can strain relationships, as partners grapple with the balance between their own aspirations and societal norms.

Strategies for Managing External Pressures:

1. Open Dialogue: Engage in transparent conversations about the societal and cultural pressures you're both facing. Understand each other's perspectives and feelings about these expectations.

2. Clarify Priorities: Determine your shared values and priorities as a couple. Align your decisions with what matters most to you both, rather than succumbing to external pressures.

3. Set Boundaries: Establish boundaries that protect your relationship from external influences. Make it clear to others that you make decisions as a team and will prioritize your relationship's well-being.

4. Cultivate Resilience: Develop emotional resilience to external pressures by focusing on your partnership's strength and your commitment to each other.

5. Focus on Communication: Create a safe space for open communication. Discuss your concerns, fears, and dreams with each other to ensure you're both on the same page.

Reframing Perspectives:

1. Shift Your Focus: Redirect your attention from external pressures to the core of your relationship. Remind yourselves of the love, understanding, and connection you share.

2. Reevaluate Expectations: Challenge societal expectations that don't align with your values and goals. Decide what you want for your relationship and embrace choices that resonate with you both.

3. Practice Self-Compassion: Be kind to yourselves when facing external pressures. Remember that you're navigating a complex landscape, and it's okay to prioritize your well-being.

Creating a Resilient Partnership:

Chapter 11 underscores that relationships can thrive despite external pressures when partners work together to foster understanding and resilience. By recognizing that your partnership is a unique journey, independent of societal expectations, and by prioritizing open communication and shared values, you can create a sanctuary that shields your love from the storms of external influences.

In essence, navigating relationship pressures involves acknowledging the external factors while fostering an unwavering commitment to each other. By remaining anchored in your shared vision and by valuing the depth of your connection, you can transform challenges into opportunities for growth and create a bond that is resilient, authentic, and unwavering.

12

The Future of Relationships

As the world continues to evolve, so too do the dynamics of relationships. Chapter 12 delves into the fascinating realm of the future of relationships, reflecting on the changing landscape and offering insights into potential trends and strategies to navigate the challenges that lie ahead.

Evolving Nature of Relationships:

The future holds a promise of even greater diversity in relationship dynamics. As traditional norms continue to shift, relationships are becoming more inclusive of various forms, such as non-monogamous partnerships, long-distance connections, and relationships formed across digital platforms.

Potential Trends in Relationships:

1. Emphasis on Individuality: Partners are increasingly valuing personal growth and individuality within relationships, recognizing that fulfilling personal aspirations contributes to a strong partnership.

2. Digital Intimacy: Technology will continue to play a vital role, facilitating connections across distances and enriching relationships through virtual experiences.

3. Expanded Definition of Family: Families may extend beyond blood ties, incorporating chosen families and supportive communities that offer diverse sources of love and connection.

4. Sustainability in Relationships: Partnerships will focus more on emotional sustainability, cultivating strong bonds that endure through challenges.

5. Continual Learning: Relationships will emphasize ongoing communication and learning to adapt to partners' evolving needs and aspirations.

Strategies for Navigating the Future:

1. Open-Mindedness: Embrace the diversity of relationships that the future holds. Be open to various forms of partnership that resonate with your values.

2. Adaptability: As relationships evolve, remain adaptable to change. Continually reassess and adjust your partnership based on both partners' growth.

3. Digital Balance: Use technology to enhance connections, but also prioritize in-person interactions to foster deeper emotional intimacy.

4. Prioritize Communication: The foundation of future relationships will be rooted in transparent and open communication. Regularly engage in conversations about individual and shared goals.

5. Mutual Growth: Strive for partnerships that support individual growth while fostering a shared journey of mutual development.

Navigating Challenges Ahead:

1. External Pressures: Future relationships may still grapple with societal and cultural pressures. Stay focused on your partnership's values and prioritize each other's well-being.

2. Balancing Autonomy and Connection: As individuality becomes more valued, find the balance between pursuing personal aspirations and maintaining emotional closeness.

3. Digital Overload: While technology can enhance connections, be cautious not to let it replace genuine in-person interactions.

4. Changing Definitions: Embrace evolving definitions of family and partnership, celebrating the uniqueness of your relationship journey.

Embracing a Dynamic Future:

Chapter 12 underscores that the future of relationships is marked by adaptability, openness, and a commitment to growth. Partnerships will continue to evolve as individuals explore new ways of connecting and finding meaning. By embracing change, valuing open communication, and fostering emotional intimacy, couples can create relationships that thrive in the ever-evolving landscape of the future.

Conclusion: Navigating Modern Relationships with Resilience and Intention

The journey through the intricate landscape of modern relationships has been a remarkable exploration of the challenges, rewards, and strategies that define the way we connect in today's world. From the complexities of technology to the evolution of gender roles, from the depths of intimacy to the pressures of societal expectations, each chapter has illuminated a facet of modern love that shapes our experiences and interactions.

RELATIONSHIPS IN THE MODERN WORLD: CHALLENGES AND SOLUTIONS

Key Takeaways:

As we reflect on the insights garnered from these pages, several key takeaways emerge:

1. Open Communication: The cornerstone of any healthy relationship is open and honest communication. It's a conduit through which partners share their hopes, dreams, fears, and vulnerabilities.

2. Adaptability: The ability to adapt to change is essential in today's ever-evolving world. Successful relationships embrace change as an opportunity for growth, rather than a challenge to be feared.

3. Balanced Autonomy: Embracing individuality while maintaining emotional closeness requires a delicate balance. Both partners' aspirations and well-being deserve equal attention.

4. Technology's Role: Technology can enhance connections but should never replace genuine, in-person interactions. Mindful use of technology strengthens relationships.

5. Emotional Resilience: The journey of self-care and emotional resilience enriches partnerships. Individuals who prioritize their well-being contribute positively to their relationship's vitality.

6. Equality and Understanding: Fostering equality in relationships requires ongoing dialogue, collaboration, and respect for each other's aspirations and contributions.

Thriving Solutions for Modern Relationships:

To navigate the complexities of modern relationships with grace and resilience, consider these solutions:

1. Prioritize Communication: Establish open communication as a constant practice. Share your thoughts, feelings, and concerns openly and without judgment.

2. Embrace Change: Approach change with curiosity rather than trepidation. Adaptation allows relationships to evolve and thrive.

3. Celebrate Individuality: Encourage each other's personal growth and honor individual aspirations. Thriving relationships are built on the foundation of two strong, fulfilled individuals.

4. Cherish In-Person Moments: While technology connects us, prioritize meaningful in-person experiences that nurture emotional intimacy.

5. Support Mental Well-Being: Prioritize mental health and well-being for both partners. A resilient partnership is built on strong emotional foundations.

6. Cultivate Equality: Create an atmosphere of equality and mutual understanding. Prioritize collaboration, shared decision-making, and respect for each other's contributions.

Approach with Open-Mindedness:

As you journey forward in your own relationships, remember that no two paths are the same. Embrace the lessons shared within these chapters, and approach each day with adaptability, open-mindedness, and a commitment to genuine connection. Modern relationships are a canvas for creating bonds that flourish amidst the challenges and opportunities that life presents.

In an era defined by change, technology, and diverse expressions of love, it's your willingness to evolve, your dedication to communication, and your passion for mutual growth that will ensure your relationship's success. So, stride forth with confidence, armed with the wisdom you've gained, and paint a masterpiece of love, understanding, and resilience on the canvas of your modern relationship.

www.ingramcontent.com/pod-product-compliance
Lightning Source LLC
LaVergne TN
LVHW010439070526
838199LV00066B/6095